(GREENHILL, BASIL, AND GIFFARD, ANN)
VICTORIAN AND EDWARDIAN MERCHANT
STEAMSHIPS FROM OLD PHOTOGRAPHS £4.95

387.24

387.
24
GRE

Victorian and Edwardian

MERCHANT STEAMSHIPS

from old photographs

BASIL GREENHILL

AND

ANN GIFFARD

B T BATSFORD LTD
LONDON

for Edward and Joan Fursdon

ALSO BY BASIL GREENHILL AND ANN GIFFARD

Westcountrymen in Prince Edward's Isle
(American Association Award: Filmed: Televised)
The Merchant Sailing Ship: A Photographic History
Travelling by Sea in the Nineteenth Century
Women Under Sail
Victorian & Edwardian Sailing Ships
Victorian & Edwardian Ships and Harbours

BY BASIL GREENHILL:

The Merchant Schooners (2 volumes)
Sailing for a Living
Out of Appledore (with W J Slade)
Boats and Boatmen of Pakistan
Steam and Sail (with Rear Admiral P W Brock)
Westcountry Coasting Ketches (with W J Slade)
A Victorian Maritime Album
The Coastal Trade (with Lionel Willis)
A Quayside Camera
Archaeology of the Boat
Edited and Prefaced: The Last Tall Ships, by Georg Kåhre

First published 1979
Copyright © Basil Greenhill and Ann Giffard 1979
Printed in Great Britain by
The Anchor Press Ltd, Tiptree, Essex
for the publishers B T Batsford Ltd,
4 Fitzhardinge Street, London W1H 0AH.

ISBN 0 7134 0592 9

FRONTISPIECE:

The *Meiji Maru*, an iron steamer of 1,027 tons gross, with
engines of 1,530 indicated horsepower, is a survivor of the
great days of Victorian steamships. Built to the order of
the Japanese Government by R Napier & Sons at Glasgow in
1874, she was delivered to Yokohama in February 1875 by Captain
Robert H Peters, and served the Japanese Government as a lighthouse
tender. In 1894 she was chosen to carry the Emperor Meiji for the
first voyage ever made by an Emperor of Japan other than in a
warship. She now lies preserved in a dock alongside the
Maritime University in Tokyo.

CONTENTS

ACKNOWLEDGEMENTS

The Authors and Publishers would like to thank the following for permission to use the photographs in this book:
National Maritime Museum: Nos 1, 3, 4, 5, 6, 7, 8, 9, 10, 11, 12, 13, 14, 15, 16, 17, 18, 19, 20, 21, 22, 23, 24, 25, 26, 27, 28, 29, 30, 32, 33, 34, 36, 37, 38, 39, 40, 41, 42, 43, 44, 45, 46, 47, 48, 49, 50, 51, 52, 55, 56, 57, 58, 59, 60, 61, 62, 63, 64, 65, 66, 67, 68, 70, 71, 72, 73, 74, 76, 78, 79, 80, 83, 84, 85, 86, 88, 91, 92, 97, 98, 99;

Greenwich Borough Museum: No. 87;

Handels-og Sjøfartsmuseum, Helsingør: No. 54;

Harland and Wolff: No. 31;

Public Archives of Canada: No. 95;

Public Archives of Newfoundland: Nos 35, 69, 93;

Captain Bradford: No. 75;

R Cock: Nos 81, 82, 94;

Miss M E Giffard: No. 53.

The frontispiece and Nos 2, 77, 89, 90, 96 and 102 are the property of Basil Greenhill and Ann Giffard. Nos 100 and 101 are from the collection of B T Batsford.

INTRODUCTION

A great deal has been published in recent years about merchant sailing ships. They were among the most beautiful of man's purely utilitarian creations. They lingered on until the middle of the twentieth century and latterly they attracted the attention of photographers, so that there are many thousands of photographs of sailing ships of all kinds, some of which are reproduced in a companion volume to this one, *Victorian and Edwardian Sailing Ships*.

Although the merchant sailing ship developed literally out of all recognition in the later Victorian era, she was obsolete by the beginning of the Edwardian period. After the turn of the century only two or three dozen sailing vessels, from ketches to steel four-masted barques – see the illustrated definitions in *Victorian and Edwardian Sailing Ships* – were built in Britain, and only three or four after the death of King Edward VII.

The reasons for this great change at sea are very complex and involve such factors as the scale of industrial production and consumption, the development of the iron and later the steel industry, the development of engineering, the development of land communications and of the telegraph and telephone, the development of dock and harbour facilities all over the world and of coal bunker ports. The largest single factor – closely linked with those already listed – was the development, under the stimulus of general industrial change, of the steamship.

Experiments with steam propulsion at sea were made very early in the nineteenth century and the story of them has been told many times. On short runs wooden paddle steamers with simple low-pressure engines, even though their boilers consumed prodigious quantities of coal for the amount of cargo and/or the number of passengers they carried, could pay their way, partly because they achieved an unheard-of regularity and reliability of service, and this was important to passengers. The steam packet sailing across the channel or around the coast was, in fact, the first vehicle to travel steadily and reasonably quickly and to leave, and usually to arrive, on time. She marked the very beginnings of modern travel. By 1826 there were wooden paddle steamers in trade between Britain and Portugal. By 1837, the year of Queen Victoria's accession, the *Cape Breton* had made her pioneer steam-assisted crossing of the North Atlantic and there had been several other ocean voyages by vessels using steam engines to help their sails, including the remarkable voyage of the *Enterprise* to India. In the same year the nascent Peninsular & Oriental Steam Navigation Company, the P & O, today the world's largest shipping concern, was advertising a fortnightly service from London to Oporto, Lisbon, Gibraltar and Malaga. But it was a service which depended for its success on an effective non-commercial subsidy – the mail contract. Without the £29,600 per year paid by the

1 The *Clio*, built in 1873, owned by the Bristol Steam Navigation Company and used by them in their trade from Bristol to the continent, is here seen in the Avon Gorge on her way to Bristol City Docks. Notice the hobbler in his boat alongside and the barges and hobblers' boats lower down the river coming up on the tide. The hobblers' job was to assist with mooring lines, etc, when the vessel was docked.

Government to the company to carry the mails, wooden paddle steamers with simple engines working at the low pressures which were all that could be generated by the boilers of the day (given the state of iron founding and engineering) needed so much coal to fire those boilers to generate the steam that a large part of the cargo space had to be given over to fuel. They could not compete with sailing vessels – even though the latter could take six weeks to go to Lisbon and back, against the steamers' predictable six or seven days and constant record of three round voyages with paying cargo to the one of the sailing vessels.

This situation continued right through the era of the steam packet company – virtually until the 1860s. Slowly the steamships were improved. But to compete in general world trade with sailing vessels, three things were needed.

The first was a more efficient means of propulsion than the paddle. This was provided by the screw propeller which began to appear in the late 1830s. But the screw propeller was driven through a shaft running nearly half the length of the vessel. Wooden ships were always flexible structures built up of thousands of small pieces of timber secured together with fastenings, partly or wholly of metal, which cost a not inconsiderable fraction of the total construction cost of the vessel. As should be expected of such structures, they leaked continuously unless they were built to a standard which made them scarcely economic as cargo carriers. Add to their natural characteristics the stresses and strains produced by the torque imposed by the transmission of any reasonable amount of power through the shaft to the screw from the engine and the working life of the hull was liable to be difficult, expensive, and short.

So the second requirement became obvious – the successful steam vessel would be an iron vessel. But until the 1840s iron was not available commercially in the quantities and sizes needed to build ships of tonnages large enough to carry enough fuel to make ocean voyages. And when iron became available in the early 1840s the third requirement was still not met – there was no economical engine and the engines available continued to eat coal in vast quantities, or rather the furnaces did.

Thus at the beginning of the age of photographs the situation was that big screw-driven iron steamships could be built, but without subsidy they still could not compete with sailing vessels because their engines consumed too much fuel to leave enough room for cargo. The first photographs in the first two sections of this book illustrate the situation exactly. The *Great Britain* (Plates 4, 5, 6) of 1843 is of the greatest historical importance because she was the first big iron screw-propelled steamship and it was with her descendants that the future lay. The *Iris* (Plate 54) was a typical wooden paddle steamer of the same period, making a living on a short-range service in which she did not have to carry so much coal that she had little room left for cargo and passengers.

These photographs were taken in the 1840s and there the development of the steamship stood – to simplify – more or less still for twenty years. The short-range steamer could pay her way around the coasts and in restricted waters and did so very well in the coastal coal and ore trades and in the carrying of live cattle to the continent. The long-range steamer could not compete with sailing vessels in general world trade. Such were her operating costs in relation to her cargo and passenger-carrying capacity that she needed the effective subsidy of a mail contract to pay her way. Fortunately, such were her advantages that mail contracts were issued and bitterly fought for. Under the stimulus of the mail contract system, passenger and cargo services across the Atlantic and to the east steadily developed and while they did so the relevant parts of the British merchant shipping industry gained invaluable experience in the building and operation of steamships, experience which no other nation was acquiring at the same time. In addition, at the same time some auxiliary steamships, using their crude engines to back up the sails with which they were fully equipped, were successfully operated on long passages.

Meanwhile sailing vessel owners, in a world in which trade was unsteadily expanding, felt little competition. The standard sailing ship of 1860, which made up the great majority of British tonnage, was little different in appearance from that of 1820 and she was still basically the vessel of which the revolutionary development in a few decades of the fifteenth century had made possible the opening up of the world to western man. She was built of wood with a burdensome hull, with flat floors to enable her to take the ground in the numerous tidal harbours of Britain which still dried out twice a day; she was of from 200–800 tons and she was square-rigged with three masts as a full-rigged ship or barque – see again the illustrated definitions in *Victorian and Edwardian Sailing Ships*.

She, the traditional sailing vessel of four centuries of European expansion, bore no resemblance whatsoever to the steam vessels which were about to begin to take over the bulk of world trade from her, and very little to the sailing vessels, huge steel four-masted barques and multi-masted schooners, which were to develop to carry for three decades the steadily diminishing cargoes the steamer could not economically carry. These latter-day sailing vessels, which operated successfully for only thirty years or so, are today too often thought of as typical sailing ships of history.

The 1860s were the critical period. At the beginning of them the wooden three-masted, square-rigged sailing vessel was the unchallenged normal carrier, as she had been for centuries. At the end of the 1860s the sailing vessel in any form was obsolescent.

As early as 1856 the Pacific Steam Navigation Company was operating two vessels equipped with a new kind of steam engine. It had two cylinders, and, in simple terms, the steam was admitted first to the smaller of the two, where it achieved a portion only of its expansion, and then to the second, larger, cylinder where its expansion was completed. In each cylinder, of course, the expansion of the steam drove down the piston which transmitted the power to the crank shaft. The result of the double expansion in this compound engine was to achieve a far greater horsepower from a pound of steam and therefore from a pound of coal.

In the early 1860s, when the tiny fleet of untypical and (ever since) much over-publicised merchant sailing ships, the British China tea clippers, was being built up because the efficient American merchant shipping industry which had previously dominated the trade had been destroyed by the Civil War, never to recover, the sailing ships in the tea trade were in fact clearly already doomed. Alfred Holt of Liverpool was having built, in a yard next door to one turning out tea clippers, three compound-engined steamships with engines so efficient that they could carry a cargo of 3,000 tons (two to three times as much as most contemporary sailing vessels) and at the same time sufficient coal to drive them at a steady ten miles per hour for 8,500 miles without refuelling. Comparable clear landmarks in the history of man were the invention of the three-masted sailing ship itself, and the building of the DC2 aircraft, which began modern air transport, in the early 1930s.

The three Holt ships, the *Agamemnon,* the *Ajax* and the *Achilles,* operated on boiler pressures of 60 lb per square inch and a coal consumption of $2\frac{1}{4}$ lb per horse-power per hour. Early steamers had operated on 3–5 lb per square inch and burned as much as 10 lb of coal per horsepower per hour. From now on steam pressures rose further and coal consumption dropped. The *Achilles* (Plate 55) could steam comfortably and regularly to China in 65 days from London as against crack tea clipper time of an uncertain 90 days. She could do so with three times the cargo and she needed no subsidy. It was in this special premium trade with China tea, with its high freights, that steam was first put into direct competition on an equal footing with sail in long-range trade and the result was dramatic. The little group of clippers, typical no more of the great majority of their contemporary sailing vessels than they were of those which preceded them or those which were to follow, was still-born. As one authority has said, 'What was the use of the clipper, when the cargo steamer was already born?'. It is interesting that, whereas the story of clippers has been told and told again until even with its fictional padding it is quite threadbare, the great majority of the sailing vessels of the 1860s have been ignored and the great human achievement of the steamers that at one stroke made all large sailing vessels obsolescent is almost unknown, and only now being commemorated in new displays at the National Maritime Museum.

Perhaps one of the most dramatic demonstrations of the qualities of the compound engine was in another tea trade which also played its part in the doom of the clipper. The tea gardens of Assam in India were opened up in the early 1860s and at once cheaper tea began to become widely popular in Britain. The opening up of Assam was made possible by the river paddle steamers of the India General Steam Navigation Co, which operated on the Brahmaputra and its tributaries. When, in the early 1870s, compound engines were introduced into their vessels, the spectacular result was that fuel consumption was almost immediately halved.

The success of the Holt ships led to the steady introduction of compound engines into merchant ships generally, both new constructions and older vessels which were converted. The story is complex, for the building of iron sailing ships was developing at the same time as the compound engine steamer. In 1860, 64,700 tons of shipping were built of iron in Britain as against 147,000 tons of wooden ships. But, in addition to the home product, many wooden sailing vessels were built in the maritime provinces of Canada for sale to British owners. By 1870, 255,000 tons of iron shipping was built in Britain, as against 161,000 tons of wooden construction and the number of wooden sailing ships built in Canada for British owners was declining rapidly. By 1880 the revolution was nearly complete: 495,500 tons of iron ships were built in Britain, as against 20,000 tons of wooden shipping, and only about one-fifth of the iron tonnage comprised sailing vessels.

The day of the wooden sailing ship, only a generation before still the most economical form of long-range sea transport, was over. Her demise was almost as fast as her development had been in the shadows of the fifteenth century. Most of the 20,000 tons of wooden shipping built in 1880 in Britain were schooners and ketches, small vessels still efficient and competitive in certain ocean trades, and in the home trade, which had replaced the big smacks and the square-rigged vessels, brigs and small barques, of the early Victorian period. The big wooden sailing ship was to have only one line of development.

Between 1880 and 1910, according to their historian, Captain W J Lewis Parker, USCG, 321 four-masted schooners, 45 five-masters, and 10 six-masters, besides hundreds of three-masters, were built on the east coast of the United States. Many big wooden multi-masted schooners were also built in maritime Canada and some on the west coast of the continent. The majority of these vessels were larger than the wooden square-rigged ships of the 1860s. Some were very much larger. One was the largest wooden merchant ship ever built anywhere in the world, while a steel schooner built in 1902 was the largest sailing ship ever built at all. These wooden sailing vessels were launched because they made money. They were the most efficient and economical sailing vessels ever constructed, needing fewer men in relation to cargo carried on each passage than any of their contemporaries, steam or sail. The building of them ceased in 1907, but the wooden sailing ship had a brief revival when, during and immediately after the First World War, over 600 big vessels were built for owners in maritime Canada, the United States, Scandinavia and Finland, including four completely traditional wooden barques and a wooden full-rigged ship. But today only three wooden square-rigged merchant sailing vessels remain, the barques *Sigyn* at Åbo in Finland, *Charles W Morgan* at Mystic in Connecticut, and the steam auxiliary *Discovery* in London.

During the 1870s, though the wooden sailing vessel was much reduced in numbers, new and revolutionary changes, comparable with those taking place in steamships, enabled the iron sailing vessel to continue to compete with compound-engine steamships in a slowly but steadily decreasing number of trades.

Iron hulls were followed by iron masts and yards with iron wire standing and some running rigging. Maintenance was cut from a continuous desperate battle to a routine. The endless pumping of the wooden ship was eliminated. Steam deck engines raised the larger sails and the rigging was simplified and altered until the standard big sailing vessel became a four-masted barque many times the size of its predecessors, faster, much less liable to weather damage, with double the space for cargo in proportion to tonnage and manned by about one-third of the number of men of the wooden ships. In the 1870s, while the compound steam engine was steadily establishing itself, and the worldwide pattern of coaling stations was beginning to be built up, these new sailing vessels carried the growing trade in bulk commodities, like jute and coal, iron rails and rice, Australian and American wheat, wool from Australia and nitrate fertiliser from the west coast of South America. Soon, in the 1880s, such vessels were built of steel and became even more efficient in comparison with their wooden ancestors. On the east coast of the United States the wooden schooners were given steam hoisting engines and changes to the rigging until a four-master carrying over a thousand tons of cargo could be handled by eight men of whom only half needed to be skilled seamen.

But as the pattern of bunkering stations spread over the world and steam pressures steadily rose and with them the efficiency of engines, sailing vessels became more and more the carriers of cheap bulk cargoes – including coal for the steamer's bunkers. The steamship prospered greatly in the Black Sea grain trade, the Spanish iron ore trade, and some parts of the vast coal trade and in choice trades with perishable or costly cargoes where high freights prevailed. But after a time the compound-engined steamship reached a plateau of development and such was the expansion of the bulk trades that the sailing vessel remained in great numbers, the coal for the steamers and developing world industry gave her more and more of her cargoes, while wheat from North America and Australia provided perhaps the bulk of the rest. In 1882, 550 sailing vessels were employed in the grain trade from the west coast of North America to Europe. Similar vessels in large numbers sailed in the Australian grain trade and the great rice trade from the Bay of Bengal.

The big American schooners traded widely, but their principle employment was in carrying coal from the loading ports in the south, especially in Virginia, to New York and to New England ports for the factories and fires of the growing industrial urban areas.

But in the 1880s a second revolution occurred and the delicate balance established between steam and sail was rapidly and forever upset in favour of the former. When the compound-engined steamship seemed to have settled at the limits of its possibilities, another development as dramatic as that marked by the introduction of the *Agamemnon* and her sisters in the early 1860s marked the establishment of the steamship as the normal method of sea transport and brought about the utter demise of the large sailing vessel.

This second revolution had its preliminaries. Iron plates were cheap in the 1870s, but steel for shipbuilding was expensive. There was an enormous demand for steel for other industrial purposes, and particularly for railway development throughout the world. But by the end of the 1870s steel was being used for boilers and furnace construction and this meant that steam pressures could be increased, with further consequent improvement to the efficiency of the compound engine – and fuel consumption was reduced by more than 60 per cent.

As the *Achilles* and her sisters of 1864 marked the end of the more than four centuries-long domination of the three-masted square-rigged wooden sailing ship, so the sailing of the *Aberdeen* from Plymouth towards Melbourne on 7 April 1881 marked the beginning of the end of the big sailing ship in any form.

The *Aberdeen,* built in Glasgow, had an engine in which the steam, having done its work in the second cylinder of the compound engine, was admitted to a third cylinder even larger than the second, and there completed its expansion. This process was made possible by the high steam pressures obtained from steel boilers and improved furnaces. The *Aberdeen* completed her passage to Melbourne in 42 days with 4,000 tons of cargo and only one coaling stop, working at a steam pressure of 125 lb per square inch. But in three years 150 lb steam pressure had been reached. In 1885 two-cylinder compound engines ceased to be built. In 1887 ordinary working steam pressure passed 150 lb and shortly reached 200 lb. By the beginning of the 1890s a tramp steamer could operate at 9 knots on a fuel consumption of half an ounce of coal per ton per mile steamed. This statistic has been put in vivid terms – a first-class cargo steamer of the last years of Queen Victoria's reign could carry one ton of cargo one mile using heat in her furnace equivalent to that generated by burning one sheet of high quality Victorian writing paper. There were similar revolutionary improvements in the economics of the operation of ships which were predominantly passenger carriers and of the cargo liners which now began to appear. It was a very long way from the performance of the *Queen of the South* of less than 2,000 tons which had consumed 4,684 tons of coal on one passage from Britain to Calcutta in the 1850s. Today, of course, efficiencies are even greater and a container carrier built in the 1970s can carry one ton for 500 miles on one gallon of fuel oil – and at 21 knots.

This technical miracle of the Victorian era not only established the British merchant shipping industry as supreme in the world until the débâcle which began in 1914; it meant that Britain became wedded to steam and perhaps unduly tardy in the adoption of diesel power when that third revolution occurred in the first generation of the twentieth century. The triumph of the steamship, aided by sundry other developments – the introduction of water ballast, improved ships' cargo handling gear, bigger hatches following on improvements in construction, improved port facilities giving an even quicker turn round and increased utilisation to the efficient and expensive steam vessels, the introduction of self-trimming bulk carriers, the substitution of oil fuel for coal which made possible the better control of combustion in the furnaces and even greater engine efficiency, the growth in size of industry and with it of ships with the attendant economies of scale – was complete. In 1906 the last big sailing ships were built in Britain for British owners, and new construction had been a very thin trickle for five or six years before that.

The small sailing ship, the wooden schooner and ketch as she had developed in the second half of Queen Victoria's reign, was little affected by these dramatic developments. The compound-engined steamship could not be built economically in sizes which gave her serious competition in many of her trades. So the sailing ship ended as she had begun – as a small wooden vessel, operating over limited ranges in trades involving the movement of small parcels of cargo. She continued to be built in Britain until the First World War, in North America until the late 1920s, in Denmark and Spain until the Second World War and even after. Her supplanters were the small motor ship and, even more, the development of road transport, the rising costs of labour, the development of alternative occupations and more acceptable forms of employment ashore in the communities which had operated

2 A view looking aft along the open decks of the *Meiji Maru*. Now 104 years old, she is perhaps the only survivor in the world of her era.

small wooden sailing vessels, and the whole pattern of twentieth-century manufacture, packaging, marketing and distribution.

We are most grateful to Denis Stonham, who is in charge of the National Maritime Museum's Historic Photograph Archive, for his help in assembling the photographs in this book and to Robin Craig of University College, London, Captain W J Lewis Parker, USCG, and Captain Neville Upham, for invaluable historical advice.

Note on the horsepower rating of marine steam engines

The work output of a marine engine is usually expressed in horsepower, but due to the variety of machinery used in vessels of various types a different horsepower may be used in stating a particular vessel's power output.

In the case of the steam reciprocating engine the pressure of steam on the piston of the engine is measured by a device known as an *indicator*. The indicator is attached to a special cock on the engine cylinder, and as the engine stroke is completed a banana-like graph is drawn on a paper mounted on a revolving cylinder.

The horsepower obtained from the indicator diagram is termed the *indicated horsepower,* the actual power output of the engine is, however, less than the ihp and is termed the brake horsepower (bhp). This is measured at the shaft by using a type of brake termed a dynamometer. The horsepower of oil engines is frequently expressed in bhp, though it is usual for the marine engineer to measure at regular intervals its ihp as with a steam reciprocating engine.

In a turbine it is not possible to measure indicated horsepower by taking an indicator diagram from the working cylinder as in a reciprocating engine. The usual method of obtaining the power developed is to measure the twist of the propeller shaft. To achieve this a *torsion* meter is employed to determine a figure from which calculations give the shaft horsepower of the engine (shp).

Nominal horsepower is an arbitrary figure, arrived at by using a formula which was developed by James Watt in the very early period of the development of the steam engine, to give a measure of engine performance. Due to technological advances in the steam engine, a formula, even as early as 1875, had almost become meaningless. (For example the National Maritime Museum's paddle tug *Reliant* has an nhp of 80 against an ihp of 400). It is, however, traditionally retained for formal purposes.

PASSENGER STEAMERS

The Victorian and Edwardian eras saw the passenger steamer, both the ocean liner and the short sea packet boat, the ferry to the continent or to Ireland develop from its very beginnings to what might be considered its finest stage.

When Queen Victoria came to the throne there were already a number of more or less regular steam services around the coasts of Britain and across the Channel. In 1833 the *Cape Breton* had made the historic first steam-assisted crossing of the North Atlantic – and in the difficult east to west direction. A few years later the *Great Western* inaugurated mail-contract-subsidised regular trans-Atlantic services and a new era in which for the first time the passenger at sea was an important commercial asset, to be treated as such. At the end of the Edwardian era the oceans of the world were criss-crossed with passenger steamship routes, and travel by sea had become perhaps the most luxurious form of passenger transport which has ever existed in any age.

Almost all passenger steamers carried cargo in varying quantities from subsidised mail to large quantities of goods or raw materials. It is not always easy to distinguish vessels by function. A few steamers illustrated in this section carried so much cargo that they could almost equally well have been placed in the next, among the cargo steamers, and vice versa. The real distinction is between liners – vessels running to a regular schedule with either passengers or cargo or both – and tramps which carried cargo where it paid them to do so, and a few passengers, often, from time to time.

3 PREVIOUS PAGE The handsome *City of Rome* was built in 1881 and sailed in the service from Liverpool to New York, and later from Glasgow to New York, for twenty years. She carried 520 first-class and 810 third-class passengers and in 1898 she was used for the repatriation of 1,690 Spanish officers and men to Santander after the Spanish American war. She is here shown off Liverpool.

4 This photograph was made by Fox Talbot in 1843 and shows the steamship *Great Britain* lying in Bristol Docks shortly after her launch. It is quite probable that this was the first photograph ever to be taken of a ship of any kind and the negative is now one of the treasures of the National Maritime Museum. The development of the big iron- or steel-built, propeller-driven, ocean-going steamship, which was to become the vehicle of Britain's dominance of the seas before the First World War, really began with the *Great Britain*. Designed by Brunel for the trans-Atlantic passenger service, this remarkable vessel had two of the three essential prerequisites for the successful steamship – a metal hull and a screw propeller. The third ingredient for viability, an economical engine, was to come twenty years later.

5 The *Great Britain* was the first large iron ship. In 1853, after a number of voyages across the Atlantic, she was refitted as a full-rigged sailing ship. She was equipped with an oscillating engine of 500 nominal horsepower and she had a long and successful career as a steam auxiliary passenger and cargo vessel running between Britain and Australia, making some thirty round voyages between 1853 and 1876.

6   In 1886 after weather damage off Cape Horn the *Great Britain* was made into a storage hulk in the Falkland Islands, where she is seen in this photograph. In 1970 this landmark in the history of ships was brought back to Bristol. Her restoration, the most ambitious project of its kind going forward anywhere in the world, is now well under way, and she may be viewed by visitors in the drydock in which she was built nearly a century and a half ago.

7   Much more typical of the passenger steamers of the early Victorian era was the elegant *Ripon,* an iron side-paddle steamer. Built in 1846 she worked the Southampton to Alexandria section of the Peninsular & Oriental Steamship Company's India and Far Eastern Service. Even in the late 1850s, despite the success of screw steamers, the paddle was still considered the best means of propulsion for this kind of fast, relatively short-range, subsidised passenger service.

8   The P & O liner *Simla* was an iron-screw vessel built in Glasgow in 1854 and used by the P & O on their service from Suez to Aden, Point de Galle in Ceylon, and Madras and Calcutta. Like all the steamers of her time, she is heavily rigged, in her case as a three-masted schooner, and has a hull shape reminiscent of the later iron and steel sailing vessels.

9 PREVIOUS PAGE The very handsome barque-rigged iron-screw steamship *Ceylon* was built at Poplar, London, in 1858 for the P & O and employed by them on a number of routes including that from Point de Galle in Ceylon to Melbourne. The hull, with its quarter galleries, graceful clipper stem and the figurehead under the bowsprit, still shows the influence of the wooden sailing vessel of the immediately preceding era.

10 The *Ceylon* had an interesting history, serving until 1907. After 1881 she was employed as a cruising vessel and her survival in this business, in which she was something of a pioneer, led to the taking of the remarkable series of detailed photographs in this and the next four plates, which, though she had probably been somewhat altered over the years, illustrate a very early passenger steamship in remarkable detail.

11 As with all early steam vessels, the *Ceylon's* accommodation was laid out like that of a contemporary sailing ship, with a continuous main deck on which houses were built in which some of the passengers and the crew lived. Unlike most sailing vessels, she did not have a raised poop deck aft, but the main passenger saloon for meals and recreation was probably situated in the stern on the deck immediately below that shown here.

12 The previous photograph of the *Ceylon* (Plate 11) was taken looking aft on the port side of the main deck. This photograph was made from approximately the same position looking forward, so that the two between them cover the whole length of the vessel. Note the sailing ship-style rigging, the deck houses, the bulwarks rather like those of a wooden ship in appearance, the funnel and the open bridge.

13 Like all vessels, steam or sail, which had long lives, the *Ceylon* was no doubt considerably altered in detail. The open bridge is typical of the period when she was built. The wheel house is probably of a later date. The joints of meat hanging in the open remain characteristic of the 1890s, when these photographs are believed to have been made, as of the 1850s, when the *Ceylon* first entered service.

14 The forward decks of the *Ceylon*. The topgallant fo'c'sle is very reminiscent of the steel sailing ships built a generation after the *Ceylon*, as is the deck house immediately abaft, with its skylight, which would have been part of the crew's accommodation in a sailing vessel.

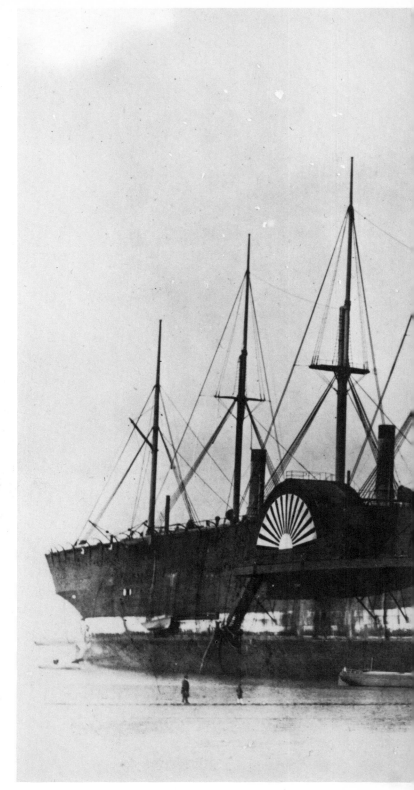

15 The *Ceylon* was a normal first-class passenger steamer of her period. The *Great Eastern,* launched in 1858 and depicted here in her old age laid up in the Mersey, was anything but normal. Her genesis lay in the idea of a steam vessel large enough to carry coal for a non-stop voyage to Australia, as well as a large number of passengers and a paying tonnage of cargo, at a time when steam engines were very inefficient and consumed vast quantities of fuel. She was roughly six times the size of any ship built before her.

16   The building of the *Great Eastern* on the Thames took
four years and excited enormous public interest. One of
the problems was to develop sufficient power to drive her.
In the end both screw and paddles were used with
separate engines. The forging of the great crank shaft for
the huge paddles was one of the major engineering
achievements of the period. This photograph was taken
during the prolonged struggle to launch the huge vessel.

17 The photograph shows the state of the *Great Eastern*
on 2 November 1857. Like the *Great Britain,* a product of
the genius of Isambard Kingdom Brunel, but an unsuccess-
ful one; the appalling problems to which she gave rise
helped to bring about his early death.

18 The *Great Eastern*'s commercial failure is a well-known story. She was never employed in the trade for which she was designed, but made her name as a cable layer. In nine years she laid five cables across the Atlantic and one from Bombay to Suez. This photograph of some of her officers and others, including women, on her bridge, was taken at this period in her career.

19 Also taken during her cable-laying years, this photograph shows very well the huge size of the *Great Eastern* and the great open area of her upper deck. This part was known as 'Oxford Street' to her cable-laying crews. The dog is probably the mastiff named Harold which belonged to Captain Robert Halpin, the highly successful master of the *Great Eastern* who laid some 26,000 miles of deep-sea telegraph cable.

20 The *Great Eastern* was not the only crack passenger liner to become a cable layer. The Cunard liner *Scotia* of 1862 was the last paddle-propelled vessel to be built for the Company. Paddles were obsolete and she was uneconomic compared with a screw steamer of the same size; but she was faster than the contemporary screw steamers and this was a very important matter with Cunard. Equipped with side lever engines like those of the tug *Reliant,* preserved in the National Maritime Museum, but of 5,000 indicated horsepower giving her a speed of 14 knots, she was a record breaker. In her old age she was stripped of her paddles and given two screws driven by compound engines and equipped as a cable layer. She is shown off Gravesend in this form on 30 June 1879. She was wrecked in 1904.

21 These four photographs demonstrate clearly the very different states of development of steam passenger vessels employed on different routes in the 1870s. The vessel shown here is the iron steam auxiliary barque *Northumberland,* built at Blackwall in 1871 and employed in the Australian passenger trade by Money, Wigram and Co. On the long run round the Cape of Good Hope the *Northumberland* made extensive use of sail as well as of her compound engine, so she was given a more or less orthodox barque rig. The photograph was taken off Gravesend on 21 September 1873.

22 Many first-class passengers are said to have preferred full-rigged auxiliary steamships like the *Northumberland* and her sister the *Durham,* shown here, built at Blackwall in 1874 and photographed a year later, to the fully powered steamships of the P & O, which, in any case, did not provide a through service to Australia for another decade. With the further development of the compound-engined steamship, however, both these ships were sold in the early 1880s to become merchant sailing vessels without engines.

23 By way of complete contrast the mail-contract-subsidised *Germanic* built of iron in 1874, the same year as the *Durham,* by Harland and Wolff for the White Star Line, was a fully powered steamship with her principal passenger space amidships, replacing the deck houses and high bulwarks of the earlier liners like the *Ceylon* (Plates 9–14) with accommodation the full width of the ship.

Thus the passenger liner was given the beginnings of the profile it was to retain for eighty years. On the relatively short North Atlantic route the *Germanic* could carry enough coal to steam at full power all the time, and it was the sails which were auxiliary, not the engines.

24 This rare photograph shows the midships deck of the *Germanic* over her main accommodation, while she was proceeding under both steam and sail. She was driven initially by two compound engines, giving her a speed of 16 knots and, with the *Britannic,* was the first liner to reduce the trans-Atlantic passage to seven and a half days. When she was seventeen years old she made a crossing in seven days seven hours and thirty-seven minutes. The first passenger liner to provide forced draught ventilation, so that passengers had some control over the temperature of their cabins, she was not broken up until 1950.

25 PREVIOUS PAGE   The handsome passenger steamer *Orient,* built at Glasgow in 1879, was very much in the tradition of the *Germanic* rather than of the *Durham*. She was a compound-engined steamship in the Australian trade for the Orient Steam Navigation Company and could carry 120 first-class, 130 second-class, and 300 third-class passengers. Her first passage to Australia took thirty-seven days and twenty-two hours.

26   The breakthrough with the compound engine was made with cargo vessels in the early 1860s – see Plate 55. The next great step forward was the introduction of the triple-expansion engine fifteen years later. The vessel concerned was the *Aberdeen,* which did not look like the world's most advanced fully powered steamship, with her pole masts and yards and the clipper bow and figurehead. She was a passenger liner with berths for forty-five first-class passengers and 650 emigrants, built by Robert Napier & Sons of Glasgow in 1881 for G Thompson & Co of Aberdeen to run to Australia. Her engine immediately became virtually the standard design for a cargo vessel until the introduction of diesel propulsion in large ships in the reign of King George V. The photograph was taken off Gravesend in 1887.

27   This photograph should be contrasted with those of the *Germanic* in Plates 23 and 24. It shows clearly the long narrow deck houses between high bulwarks – an enlarged version of the arrangements of the *Ceylon* (see Plates 9–14) – which characterised the accommodation arrangements of liners until the adoption, on the North Atlantic route, of midships' accommodation the full width of the vessel in the *Oceanic* of 1870. It was a number of years before this change was made in Far Eastern service passenger vessels. This one, the *Rome,* was built for the P & O of iron at Greenock in 1881, the same year as the *City of Rome* (Plate

28　The Allan liner *Parisian,* heavily rigged as a four-masted schooner with pole masts, is here seen at anchor in a ripping tide in the Mersey. She was the largest steel steamer afloat when she was built for the Liverpool-Canada Service in 1880/81. She was also the first North Atlantic liner to be fitted with bilge keels, which had a stabilising effect. She was given triple-expansion engines in 1899 and wireless as early as 1902. In 1912 she rescued some of the survivors of the *Titanic*.

29　The *Etruria* was built of steel by John Elder & Co of Glasgow in 1884 for the Cunard Line. She was one of the last single-screw vessels to be put on the North Atlantic express route. Capable of carrying over 1,300 passengers, in 1892 she made an Atlantic crossing in six days and twenty minutes. Note the use of sail, even in the 1890s, in first-class single-screw vessels.

30 By 1889 a revolution had taken place in external appearance of the Atlantic liner, and vessels were to remain largely of the same general appearance until the mid-twentieth century. The *Teutonic,* built in that year by Harland & Wolff for the White Star Line, was a twin-screw vessel without sails and without the sailing vessel's yards and rigging. She was also the first North Atlantic liner to be built to Admiralty requirements for use as an armed cruiser in times of war. In 1891 she held the 'Blue Riband' with a passage of 20.35 knots.

31 The *Teutonic*'s twin shafts can clearly be seen in this photograph of her, taken in drydock. Notice the beautiful eliptical counter stern, a legacy of the sailing ship design of a decade earlier. The *Teutonic* was broken up in 1921.

2 PREVIOUS PAGE   The *Orotava,* also built in 1889, but
or a different service, was less modern in her appearance
han was the *Teutonic.* She was originally intended for the
iverpool to Valparaiso route, but was transferred to the
ustralian trade almost immediately. Built at Barrow, she
as operated by the Pacific Steam Navigation Company in
ssociation with the Orient Line, working a service through
Sydney. In 1896 she capsized and sank at her berth in
ilbury with the loss of four lives, but was salved and
efitted and sent back on the Australian run.

3 LEFT ABOVE   The *Magdalena,* a much smaller passenger
d cargo vessel, was also built in 1889. She is shown in a
pical situation, discharging cargo with her own derricks
to sailing lighters in a roadstead in the Tropics – in this
se at Trinidad.

34 LEFT   The liners and cargo vessels of the Victorian and
Edwardian eras burned coal, and the development of the
steamship routes was to some extent influenced by the
gradual development of coal bunkering stations round the
world where steamers could be refuelled. The coal was
usually taken out from Britain in sailing vessels and in this
way at least the development of steamships actually
encouraged the further development of the sailing ship.
The coal was nearly always transferred from shore to ship
by manual labour – every piece being carried on board in
baskets. In Indian ports this work was done by women.
Here, at Port Said, the *Ophir,* built in 1891 at Glasgow for
the Orient Line, is being coaled from lighters. All coaling
was arduous, filthy work for everybody concerned.

35   The men who stoked the furnaces by hand had one of
the worst jobs in the history of industry. The awful heat,
the endless labour of moving coal and stoking, made much
worse in a bad sea and worse still in the Tropics, created
conditions it is difficult even to imagine today. These are
the stokers of the *Beothic,* a steamer in service with
passengers and cargo on the Newfoundland coast.

36 By way of contrast with the passenger liners which the preceding and following photographs show, this picture was taken on board a passenger vessel of a different kind. She was the *Cornwall,* built in 1896 for the Federal Steam Navigation Co, a direct descendant of Money, Wigram & Co, who had operated the *Northumberland* and *Durham* (Plates 21 and 22). Like its predecessor, the company named its ships after English counties. The *Cornwall,* here shown with a deck cargo of horses, was a single-screw steamship carrying twelve first- and 156 third-class passengers and a good deal of cargo, some in refrigerated space. She operated between England and Australia and New Zealand, usually via South Africa.

37 Despite the relative sophistication of the engineering and the luxury of the passenger accommodation, the Cunarders of the 1890s still maintained the open bridge on which the officers and their supporters had to maintain watch in all weathers. Only the quarter-master at the wheel was sheltered, and even this innovation was criticised on the grounds that it made him less vigilant – though American wooden sailing ships had had wheel houses, some of them heated, for a decade or more when the *Lucania,* shown in this and the next two photographs, was built.

38 The enormous triple-expansion engines which drove the Atlantic liners of the late Victorian and Edwardian eras were magnificent examples of the engineering of that age. This is part of the engine room of the *Lucania,* built at Glasgow in 1893 for the Cunard Line. She was of about 13,000 tons.

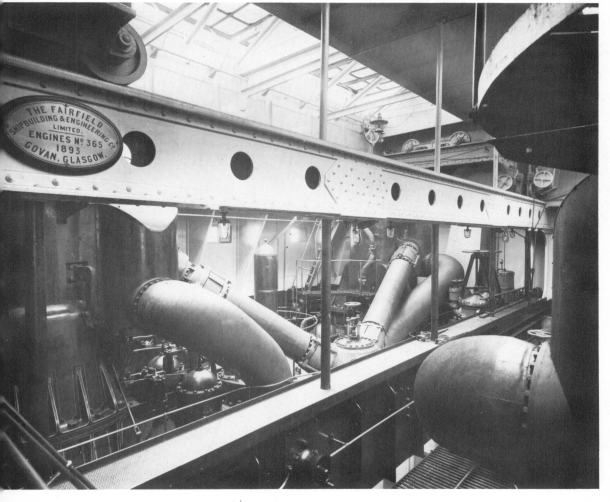

39 The accommodation of the liners of the late Victorian and Edwardian eras was magnificent in the extreme. Fortunately, many photographs survive in the National Maritime Museum which show the very high degree of luxury in which our great-grandparents could travel. This one shows the first-class dining room of the *Lucania,* decorated in what was described as 'modified Italian Style' with coffered ceiling in white and gold supported by ionic columns. The Spanish mahogany walls are richly carved with pilasters and other forms of decoration. This accommodation was one of the ultimate forms of the self-expression of a highly prosperous and confident age.

40 The *Omrah* was built for the
Orient Line six years after the
Lucania. This photograph shows the
first-class dining room, complete
with organ, massive buffet and
revolving chairs, marshalled to allow
of easy use by people of both sexes in
very formal dress. But, in comparison
with the furnishings of the *Lucania*,
these chairs have become deformed,
the backs shorter, the seats plumped
up, the arms ready to grab their
occupants. Opulence has now become
grandiose vulgarity, the classical
syntax debased to mere jargon. The
upper storey is town-hall romanesque,
the skylight built with the absolute
confidence that no heavy sea would
ever reach the high midships structure
where it stood. Only the lampshades
have a natural gaiety, and they would
be collectors' pieces now.

41   The *Saxonia* was built for the Cunard Line in 1900 and
scrapped in 1925. She was of 14,000 tons. Notice that the
upper bridge is still open and that the crew members wear
the quasi-naval uniform favoured by the crack Atlantic
passenger companies until the middle of the twentieth
century.

42   The *Saxonia* had the reputation of being a remarkably steady vessel in a seaway, which is just as well when one looks at this splendid photograph of the furnishings of the first-class dining room. Note the electric lights; the dining room is the full width of the ship and at last the furnishings have broken away from the long tables, inherited from sailing ships and illustrated in Plates 39 and 40, to tables accommodating eight passengers, with a reasonable amount of room between the heavy swivel chairs.

43   On one of her earliest passages the *Saxonia* crossed the
Atlantic with 2,260 passengers – the largest number to have
travelled from Britain to North America in one ship to that
date. Two of them were accommodated in this second-class
cabin. It is considerably better than most first-class
accommodation a generation before and is markedly better
than that offered on some North Sea ferries today. The
plaques on the decorated guard rails bear the device of the
Cunard Steam Ship Company Limited, and the metal
fittings are gleaming brass, which, in the days before
plastic lacquer, had to be regularly cleaned and polished.

44   By way of contrast with Plate 42, here is a third-class
dining space in the *Saxonia*. Even this austere compartment
represents a considerable improvement, of course, on the
third-class accommodation of only a generation before, not
the least of its benefits being the provision of a living space
separate from the sleeping berths. Moreover, these simple
fittings could be easily fumigated.

45 A year after the *Saxonia* the *Celtic,* of almost 21,000 tons, was the first vessel to exceed the tonnage of the *Great Eastern.* She was built by Harland & Wolff for the White Star Line's Liverpool to New York service and wrecked on the Irish coast in 1928.

The Allan liner *Victorian*, together with her sister the
Virginian, were not only the first turbine steamers on the
North Atlantic, but they were also the first triple-screw
steamers and among the fastest ships afloat. Built in 1904,
the *Victorian* was fitted with Parsons steam turbines, which
represented the next great technical break-through in
practical steamship propulsion after the triple-expansion
engine, demonstrated successfully in the *Aberdeen* (Plate
5). The *Victorian* could carry 1,000 first class and nearly
500 each in the second and third class. She was broken up
1929.

47 This remarkable photograph shows six steamships of
the Union Castle Line lying in dock together. They are,
from left to right, the *Goth*, the *Arundel Castle*, the
Goorkha, the *Raglan Castle*, the *Braemar Castle* and the
Gaika. These vessels maintained regular passenger and
cargo services to South Africa and their successors ceased
to carry passengers only in 1977.

48 For many people the ultimate passenger steamer will always remain the first *Mauretania*. Built in 1907 for the Liverpool-New York service of the Cunard Line by Swan Hunter on the Tyne she exceeded 30,000 tons and had quadruple screws. Her accommodation, and that of her sister the *Lusitania,* was of a standard not previously approached even on the North Atlantic service. On her second North Atlantic voyage she regained for Cunard the Blue Riband with an average speed of 23.99 knots; later she averaged well over 25 knots in the course of forty-four round voyages. She passed in due course to the Southampton-New York service and was broken up in 1935; her passing perhaps really marked the end of the Victorian and Edwardian era for passenger steamers.

BALMORAL CASTLE

49 The *Balmoral Castle* was built in 1910 for the Union Castle England–South Africa service and so represents the end of the development of the passenger liner in the Victorian and Edwardian eras. In this photograph it can be seen that she still has the open bridge, so much favoured in an age with strong memories of sailing ships and a high regard for experience in sail. She has, however, lost the yards and sails so conspicuous in the photograph of earlier Union Castle liners (Plate 47).

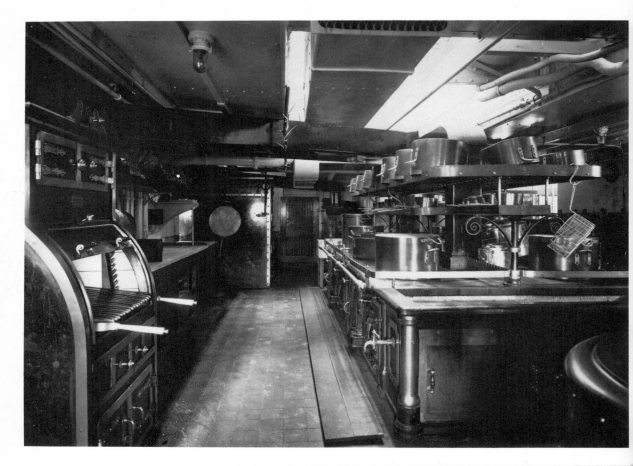

50, 51 and **52**   These three plates show accommodation and working areas in the *Balmoral Castle* at the end of Edward VII's reign. Plate 50 shows the kitchen, or in old-fashioned seafaring terms the passenger galley. Here a small army of cooks sweated without any modern conveniences to keep a constant flow of food hot and on time to the three or more dining rooms, whatever the weather conditions. Plate 51 shows a pantry with some examples of the silver and china teaware. And Plate 52 shows a third-class cabin, with four berths, simple, but quite comfortable, accommodation, even by the standards of the cheaper accommodation in cruising vessels today.

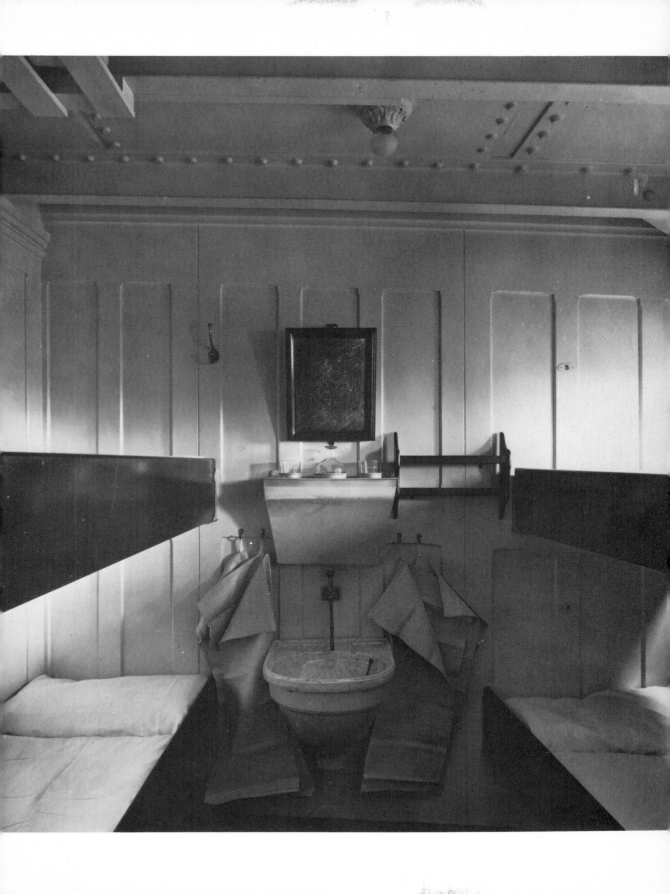

CARGO
STEAMERS

The cargo vessel, like the passenger liner, developed out of all recognition in the Victorian and Edwardian eras. From a paddle vessel which could be operated profitably only on short passages around the coast, to the continent or to Ireland, she became one of the most efficient products of nineteenth-century technology, able to steam half way round the world without refuelling. Though sailing vessels also underwent revolutionary development in later Victorian times, by the 1880s they were in relative decline and by the end of the Edwardian era in the British merchant shipping industry the big sailing vessel was obsolete.

53 PREVIOUS PAGE This photograph, taken in the early years of the Edwardian period, shows the harbour at Malaga with merchant steamships moored and discharging into, or loading from, lighters. By now masts are reduced to derricks and only one of these vessels is an old-timer with squaresails still visible on yards on the foremast.

54 This is the earliest photograph of an ordinary merchant steamship of which we know. It must have been taken in the 1840s. Strictly speaking, its subject, the *Iris*, like many other vessels straddles Sections 1 and 2 of this book, because she carried passengers as well as goods on a packet service between Danish Islands – the type of service which is still carried on by small motor ships.

The *Iris* was built by James and William Hall at Aberdeen in 1842. When she was launched, steamships, because of the limits imposed by paddle propulsion and very uneconomical simple low-pressure engines, could only really profitably be employed on short packet routes and on subsidised North Atlantic and other mail services. Shortly after she was built the *Iris* was sold to the Aalborg Steam Ship Co and for fifteen years provided an efficient packet service between Copenhagen and Aalborg.

55 The great break-through came in 1865 when the *Agamemnon,* the *Ajax* and the *Achilles* were launched for the Ocean Steamship Co, the grandfather of the great Ocean Group of today. They were all built by Scott & Co at Greenock and were each equipped with single-crank compound tandem engines developing 945 indicated horsepower. With these three steamships three technical developments of the second half of the nineteenth century were successfully combined: the iron hull, the screw propeller and the economical compound engine. In addition the Ocean Steamship Co applied relatively advanced managerial techniques in the operation of steam vessels in long-range trades.

The three vessels were placed in the China trade and their successful use in this business, steaming all the way regularly from Liverpool to Mauritius via the Cape of Good Hope, over 8,000 miles, without stopping to refuel, marked the beginning of the end of the merchant sailing ship in general long-range ocean trade.

56 The success of the *Agamemnon* and her sisters signalled not only the beginning of the end of the big merchant sailing ship but also the very beginning of the end of the era when steamships carried the masts and yards of a sailing ship to back up their engines, though the use of sail by steamships was to be a very long time dying. The *Deucalion,* also an Ocean Steamship Company vessel, and seen in this photograph in the Suez Canal, was built in 1872, only seven years after the three pioneers, but her general appearance resembles that of vessels afloat eighty years later and her greatly reduced rigging and sails are the result of a combination of reliable economical machinery and the Suez Canal route, eliminating long passages in areas of predictable winds. The *Deucalion* is shown in convoy in the Suez Canal, 'geered' to the bank to allow another convoy to pass in the opposite direction. The opening of the canal in 1869 reduced the distance from Britain to China by 3,000 miles, or ten to twelve days' steaming for the vessels of the period.

57 The *Istrian* was built for the Bibby Line's Mediterranean service by Harland & Wolff in 1867. She was taken over by the Leyland Line for their North Atlantic service and with two other vessels maintained a useful regular fortnightly schedule in the middle 1870s. Essentially a cargo rather than a passenger liner, the *Istrian* was rigged as a four-masted schooner, but with her raised deck amidships anticipated in some ways the practices of the next decade of shipbuilding. She was converted to have a compound engine in 1877.

58 The *Nestor* was built for the Ocean Steamship Co at
Hebburn in 1868 and equipped with a compound engine of
450 indicated horsepower. She was 313 feet long, bigger
than almost all contemporary sailing vessels and about the
size of the last big steel sailing ships which were launched
in the 1890s, but she had a beam of only 32 feet. The
Nestor and the other Ocean Steamship Company vessels
were put in the China tea trade in direct competition with
the much publicised clippers. By 1869, the year of the
building of the *Cutty Sark,* they had established themselves.
Their cargoes were delivered sooner and in better
condition than those of their rivals, whether steam or sail,
and sold for 2d per pound more. Alfred Holt, the presiding
genius behind these vessels, wrote in that year: 'The
clippers made their usual good passages, but the demand
for new teas was fairly over before their arrival'.

9   In the early 1860s steam communication between
Britain and New Zealand was still via a branch service
across the Tasman Sea from Australia. New Zealanders
looked to a Pacific route via the Isthmus of Panama for
improved communications. What looked like a great step
forward was taken with the establishment of the Panama,
New Zealand & Australia Royal Mail Co, which was to
maintain sailings between Panama and Sydney, via
Wellington, monthly in each direction. The *Mataura*,
shown here, was one of the first vessels in the new service.
She was an iron single-screw vessel with a compound
engine, built in 1866 at Millwall on the Thames. The route
was intended to be for both cargo and passengers, but it
was never profitable, largely because of the absence of the
intermediate ports of call which made the eastern route a
paying business, and in December 1868 the service was
abandoned. A year later the trans-continental railway
across the United States to San Francisco was completed,
and the pattern of Pacific trade began to change.

60 John Penn established a blacksmith's shop at Greenwich in 1800. He was a millwright and by 1825 he was making marine steam engines. His son, John, took over the business and made it world famous, building engines for the most advanced warships of their period, like the *Warrior* and the *Devastation,* and for many merchant ships, including early P & O vessels, at a large works occupying seven acres in Blackheath. This photograph shows a small part of the works with what looks like a shaft under manufacture in the foreground.

61 *Warwick Castle*. The brig-rigged steamship *Warwick Castle,* an early Union Castle liner, was built by R Napier & Son at Glasgow in 1877 and this photograph of her was taken at Gravesend on 7 August 1889. She had a compound engine with a nominal horsepower of 370.

62 *City of Khios*. Built in 1878 by Barclay Curle & Co the *City of Khios* is here shown in the Suez Canal. She had a compound engine of 500 nominal horsepower.

63 The *Nedjed* of Liverpool was built at Newcastle in 1883, a typical bulk cargo steamer of the period of 1,700 tons, powered with a compound engine developing 300 nominal horsepower. Notice that she still has the old-fashioned anchors with a steel stock, like the anchors of the later sailing ships, lifted over the side with hand tackles on davits. Her bridge is quite open, apart from canvas dodgers at the ends, and she has a pronounced tumble-home, that is her point of maximum beam is roughly on the loaded waterline and she narrows in above like a wooden sailing warship of the early nineteenth century.

4 and 65 These two splendid photographs show the *Bayley,* built in 1886 by Swan Hunter at Newcastle, lying off Gravesend. Although built so late, her hull resembles that of a sailing ship of the period, with its clipper bow, figurehead and bowsprit, and she is heavily rigged as a schooner. The photograph taken on board shows the midship's house with its boats, and the afterside of the bridge with a canvas dodger in place, and the furled loose-footed gaff sail on the mainmast, brailed to the mast immediately abaft the funnels, and with a cluster of engine room and stokehold ventilators around it. The *Bayley* had a triple-expansion engine of 400 nominal horsepower built by the Wallsend Slipway and Engineering Co.

66 The first steamship to be launched as a bulk oil tanker was the *Vaderland,* built by Palmers on the Tyne in 1872. Despite her German name she was owned by the Red Star Line of Philadelphia, but she did not last long in the trans-Atlantic trade for which she was designed because of objections to carrying passengers with so inflammable a cargo. It was not until 1886 that continuous development of tankers began with the *Gluckauf,* built, also on the Tyne, for German owners in 1886. The tanker shown here, the *Suwanee,* was built only two years later in 1888, an ancestor of the monster vessels which make up so much of the world's merchant shipping tonnage today.

67 The *Simonside* of Sunderland was built at West Hartlepool in 1896 of 3,000 tons and driven by a triple-expansion engine of 260 nominal horsepower. She is here shown off Gravesend on 19 September 1900, inward bound with a typical large deck cargo of timber. Cargoes like this were brought from the Baltic and Norway by the score every summer, usually in Scandinavian and Russian vessels, and by the time they reached west European ports the vessels often were floating with a pronounced list.

68 The *Clan Ferguson* was built in 1898 and, as can be
seen immediately, was a most peculiar shape. She was a
'turret' steamer, one of a group built to take advantage of
loose wording of the toll schedules of the Suez Canal. The
Canal dues were based upon measurements for tonnage, in
calculation of which ships built like this one, with narrow
decks superimposed on a hull of normal proportions,
secured an advantageous rate.

9 This magnificent photograph shows the *Grasbrook,* a
German vessel built at Hamburg in 1882, under repair in
drydock at St John's, Newfoundland. She was equipped
with a compound engine of only 190 nominal horsepower.
She was one of the smaller units of the great Hamburg
Amerikanische Packetfahrt, but little is known of her
history. With her open bridge, her burdensome hull and
the square yards on a heavily rigged foremast, she is
almost the epitome of the late nineteenth-century cargo
steamship.

STEAM
TUGS

The steam tug evolved very early in the history of the steamship and was perhaps the first really successful manifestation of the use of steam power at sea. Early steam tugs were paddle-driven vessels and paddle tugs have continued until well into the present century – a classic example is, of course, the *Reliant* preserved in the National Maritime Museum at Greenwich. The steam tug made practical the development of the large steamship, as it did also that of the last large sailing vessels, because it made it possible to handle them in the restricted waters of rivers, harbours and docks.

70 PREVIOUS PAGE This is the *Reliant,* built at Shields in 1907, a splendid example of an Edwardian paddle tug made all the more interesting by the fact that, for reasons which have not been determined, she was equipped with Victorian side-lever engines of the type used in the first passenger liners. Here she is shown hard at work as a tug.

71 This photograph shows *Three Fingered Jack,* as she was locally known, the paddle tug *Anglia,* built in 1866, lying in the Thames off Gravesend. On her starboard bow is a fine example of a North American-built wooden full-rigged ship.

72   This photograph shows the tugs *Expert* in the
immediate foreground, *Dunera,* lying on her port quarter,
and *Cambria,* the paddle tug alongside the merchant
steamship *Japan,* all photographed together off Gravesend
on 23 May 1898. The *Japan,* a P & O freighter, was built
at Greenock in 1893.

73 The tug *Nubia,* built in 1890 and here shown in the
Thames, was a handsome and very typical little vessel,
with her single sail on a diminutive mizzen mast
immediately abaft the bell top funnel. Notice her open
bridge and the two tow bows, between which two of her
crew are standing together.

74 The *Pilot* was built fifteen years after the *Nubia,* also
for Thames service. She is a much smaller tug and is here
shown with many passengers, all of them men, and flying
a number of flags for some occasion, perhaps one of the
annual races for London River sailing barges.

75 Here is the crew of a small harbour tug, an Edwardian vessel, photographed a few years after the end of the Edwardian era. They are, left to right, Reg Suthers, deckhand, Bill Seeley, deckhand, and George Roberts, driver. Captain Bradford, whose first command this was, is in the little wheel house.

76 Here is the *Reliant* (see Plate 70) as she is today, preserved in the National Maritime Museum so that you can walk her decks, visit her engine room and see the crews' quarters. She is an Edwardian steamship anyone can see. She is the largest Museum exhibit in Britain and certainly one of the most popular.

STEAM
COASTERS

During Queen Victoria's reign the steam coaster tended to a certain point to replace the small sailing vessels, first brigs and smacks and later schooners and ketches, which had carried on the all-important coasting trade around the British Isles and to nearby continental ports. But this happened only to a certain point because it was not economical to build very small steam coasters to compete with the sailing vessels and there remained many trades in which the sailing vessel predominated until the development of the motor ship, and, more important still, of lorry transport ashore.

Nevertheless the steam coaster played an important part in industrial development in the Victorian and Edwardian eras and in the development of the steamship herself, for it has been said that steam coasters were the first successful unsubsidised steamships and the pioneer steam tramps. They were a great feature of the ports of the British Isles. Usually a number could be seen steaming from any vantage point on the cliffs. They carried any kind of cargo to be moved in bulk around the coasts, feeding stuffs, grain, stone, slate, china clay, metal ores and manufactured goods.

7 PREVIOUS PAGE   A special type of small steam coaster
as the Scots puffer. These vessels evolved from the steam
arges which operated on the Forth & Clyde Canal in the
iddle of the nineteenth century which used the fresh
ater from the canal in their boilers and had no condensers,
 steam puffed out of the funnel exhaust. In due course
uffers, which had been developed into small steam
asters for use in the sheltered waters of the west coast of
otland, were fitted with compound engines and
ndensers. This photograph shows one of these little
ssels, the *Inchcolm* built in 1909 at Leith, photographed
 one of the authors in the Crinan Canal in 1946.

79   The steam coaster really became a viable proposition
with screw propulsion, and, because passages were short
and bunkers could frequently be replenished, she
developed rapidly in certain trades. This photograph
shows the *Gipsy,* built at Waterford in 1859 of iron and
equipped with an engine of 250 nominal horsepower built
in Glasgow. She ran between Bristol and Waterford in
regular packet service, but in 1878 when outward bound
for Waterford from Bristol, she grounded in the Bristol
Avon and broke her back on the ebb tide. She
demonstrated very vividly the inadequacies of the Port of
Bristol for the age of the steamship, before the new docks
at the mouth of the river were built, because she blocked
the channel into Bristol and five days after her stranding
she had to be blown up with dynamite.

8   The steam coaster first really established herself in
e trade with coal from the north-east coast to London.
rly steamers built for this trade were the *Bedlington,*
ilt at South Shields in 1842, the *Collier* of 1848, and the
hn Bowes* of 1852, built at Jarrow, shown in this
otograph. She was launched rigged as a British-style

schooner, with a square topsail on her foretopmast, but by
the time this photograph was taken her canvas was
greatly reduced. Along with many other steam vessels of
her period, and a great fleet of sailing vessels, she was
taken up as a transport during the Crimean War.

80 This photograph shows a typical steam collier of the type which carried her machinery amidships. She is the *T G Hutton,* built in 1890 at Sunderland with a triple-expansion engine with a nominal horsepower of 80. Here she is shown photographed near Gravesend in a very embarrassing situation, but one that reveals her general shape extremely well.

81 The *Test,* shown here under repair in the Richmond drydock at Appledore at the time when it was owned by R Cock & Company (this photograph came from the Cock family album), was owned in Portreath, Cornwall, by Bain Sons & Co. She was employed for some time in a trade which took her on Tuesdays with cement from London to Plymouth, then the following Friday night over to Guernsey to load stone for London, and then back to Plymouth with cement the following Tuesday, a very nice round for a steam coaster, profitable, and pleasant for the crews.

82 Also in the Richmond drydock at Appledore and from the Cock family album is this photograph of the *Pulteney*; she is a very typical vessel of her period of the raised quarter deck type with machinery aft. She was built at Troon in 1899 and owned in Falmouth where she was registered.

In the Pomona Dock at Manchester two steam coasters discharging cargo. On the right is the *Blackwater,* built Belfast in 1883 with a Scots-built compound engine of nominal horsepower, and on the left the very smart *stiff,* built a century ago in 1878 in Glasgow, with a 260 minal horsepower compound engine.

84 And finally the sole survivor and certainly the best preserved Victorian cargo steamer in Britain, the *Robin* ex *Maria* ex *Robin* built at Blackwall in 1890, and at the time of writing under restoration for the Maritime Trust as a worthy representative of all the vessels illustrated in this book.

52717

PADDLE
PASSENGER
STEAMERS

L ong after the paddle steamer had passed out of all other commercial use [in] Britain she continued to be seen in a few harbour and special service tugs, li[ke] the *Reliant,* and in vessels which carried passengers for pleasure. The princip[al] reason for this was that in tidal waters the vessels were required to have the shallow[w]est possible draft, so that they could run to a schedule using piers and wharv[es] for the maximum possible time on each tide, and they had to be highly manoeuv[er]able for coming alongside in narrow waters. In Victorian and Edwardian tim[es] highly manoeuvrable shallow-draught vessels in sheltered waters meant padd[le] propulsion. There was also an aesthetic factor. The paddle was a very visible mea[ns] of propulsion and most types of steam machinery used for driving paddles we[re] spectacular to watch in operation, so that the paddles and their engines added to t[he] pleasure seeker's enjoyment.

85 PREVIOUS PAGE This elegant paddle steamer is the *Victoria,* built in 1884, which ran a service on the south coast of Devon and the Dorset coast. She put her bows straight onto the open beach at several of her calling places, like this one in Lulworth Cove, where, in a few minutes, she will be landing passengers by means of a gang-plank rigged out from her bows, straight on to the pebbles.

86 This is a completely different type of paddle passenger steamer, the Tilbury-Gravesend ferry steamer, *Earl of Essex,* one wintry day with very few passengers on board. Steam paddle ferries like this ran ferry services in the Victorian era across a number of big rivers in Britain including the Humber and the Severn.

87 This photograph illustrates the aftermath of a tragedy. It shows the wreck of the excursion steamer *Princess Alice* which was struck by the big steamer *Bywell Castle* on 3 September 1878 in the Thames. Nearly 600 out of the 700-odd passengers on board the *Princess Alice* lost their lives. The remains of the *Princess Alice* were dragged ashore and beached and this photograph was taken shortly afterwards by Mr A Williams.

88 Another river crossed by a very frequent regular service of steam paddle ferries was the Mersey; indeed, the ferries here were a great feature of the life of Liverpool in later Victorian and Edwardian times. This photograph shows the landing stage, packed with passengers, with one full vessel about to leave and another beginning to embark its human load.

89 and **90** These two paddle steamers are of a very different kind. The British people have a taste for tea because it has been relatively cheap and easily available for over 100 years, that is, ever since the tea gardens of Assam were opened up in the 1860s. The development of these tea gardens and the transport of their product on the first stage of its journey to Europe was made possible by the river steamer services on the Brahmaputra and its tributaries. From the 1870s onwards great numbers of specially built paddle steamers, British owned and officered, ran a network of services on the rivers of East India and in the area which later became East Pakistan and is now Bangladesh.

Some vessels built in the 1880s and even before were still in service in the 1950s. These two photographs, taken by one of the authors, show three vessels of this type. They carried not only tea and jute on voyages which took them hundreds of miles up the great rivers, but also many thousands of passengers, and, provided they were not too crowded, journeys on board them were as pleasant a means of travel for all classes of passengers as can be imagined.

Besides the steam coasters, the passenger liners, the tugs and the cargo vessels, i Victorian and Edwardian times many steam vessels were built or adapted fo special purposes, for whaling, sealing, polar exploration, salvage work, cab laying and the service of lighthouses, among others. The photographs whic follow in this section illustrate some of these. They were all quite different fron their late twentieth-century equivalents.

91 PREVIOUS PAGE   A typical vessel was the very handsome whaler *Southern Cross,* built in 1886, which after years of whaling carried a very successful expedition to the Antarctic from 1898 to 1900, in the course of which for the first time ever men spent a winter on the Antarctic continent. This expedition pioneered the way for the work of Scott, Shackleton, Mawson and Amundsen. This photograph was taken at Gravesend on 29 October 1900 on the return of the *Southern Cross* from the Antarctic. She subsequently went into the Newfoundland seal fishery and was lost with all hands in 1914.

Steam whalers like the *Iceland* and the *Southern Cross* were fully rigged as sailing ships so that they could use their sails to approach the whales, because the noise of the screw frightened them and they steamed too slowly to overtake them. They used their steam in the Polar ice floes, and steam and sail together as circumstances dictated, when on ocean passages.

92   The wooden steamer *Iceland* was built at Dundee by Alexander Stephen & Son in 1872 for John Munn & Co of St John's, Newfoundland. She had a compound engine built by Pearce Bros of Dundee and she is here shown discharging seal pelts at Harbour Grace, Newfoundland. She was lost in the ice north-east of Funk Island off the Newfoundland coast in 1910. These steam sealers and whalers were built of wood because at that time it was thought that only massive wooden construction could withstand the stresses of work in the ice.

93   This photograph shows steam sealers in a completely different environment, the drydock at St John's, Newfoundland, with four of them undergoing refit after their annual battle with the ice floes during the short sealing season early in the year. These steam sealers were the last steam merchant ships to carry the masts and yards of sailing vessels. The last of them did not cease to sail until the Second World War, but this photograph was taken probably in the last year of King Edward VII's reign.

94 Another of the steam whalers and sealers to be used
in the last years of the heroic age of the exploration of the
Arctic and Antarctic was the *Nimrod,* built by Alexander
Stephen & Son at Dundee in 1866 for Job Brothers,
prominent Newfoundland merchants. She had a compound
engine, quoted as being of 60 horsepower, and it is
interesting to note that after a long voyage in another
steam sealer a contemporary wrote, 'when sailing five
knots, slow ahead with the engine, would add about one
and a half knots to the speed of our heavy vessel; sailing
even to eight knots, the propeller was of little assistance'.
The *Nimrod* was used by Sir Ernest Shackleton in 1907 on
what was to be an almost successful attempt to reach the
South Pole. She never returned to sealing but was laid up
for a period at Appledore, North Devon, where this
recently discovered photograph shows her on the mud
outside Richmond drydock. Later she was employed as a
cargo-carrying vessel and was lost on the Barber Sand off
Caister, Norfolk in January 1919 with a cargo of coal.

95 This photograph, taken in the Canadian Arctic on
board a famous Canadian steam-and-sail exploration ship
the *Arctic,* shows well the sort of conditions in which these
last rigged steamers, the last relics, if you like, of mid-
Victorian technology, still operated in the early twentieth
century.

96 Rather similar in general appearance to the steam sealers, but in fact completely different in construction and purpose was the *Lady of the Isles,* photographed by one of the authors when she was laid up in Penzance in 1935. She was, in fact, built of iron by Harvey & Co of Hayle in 1875 for the West Cornwall Steamship Co and used by them for thirty years on service from Penzance to the Isles of Scilly. She was disposed of after being ashore in 1904, but refitted and used as a salvage vessel for another thirty-five years. This veteran Victorian packet ship was finally mined during the Second World War.

97 This is a very different type of special service vessel, the little church mission launch *St Andrew* photographed off Gravesend in March 1904 with two clergymen and her crew on board. Small steam launches were in use all over the world as pleasure and service vessels before the development of the infinitely more convenient internal combustion engine.

98 This rakish-looking steamship of the first half of Queen Victoria's reign was photographed off Gravesend in 1874. She was the *Ly-Ee Moon*. She was built by the Thames Shipbuilding Company and was over 1,000 tons gross, nearly 300 feet long. Originally a paddle steamer with oscillating engines of 350 horsepower which drove her at 17 knots, a remarkable speed for the period, she was launched for the iniquitous but highly lucrative business of running opium into China from Bombay and Calcutta.

99 The Victorian and Edwardian eras were the ages of the great steam yachts of which a very fine example was the first *Sunbeam*, a large vessel 170 feet long, designed to perform equally well under steam or sail. She set nearly 8,500 square feet of canvas and was equipped with an engine delivering 350 indicated horsepower and a feathering propeller.

Owned for many years by Lord Brassey, she became world famous for the extent of her ocean voyaging, partly because her early passages were recorded by the first Lady Brassey and published in a series of books which still make very interesting reading. In 1876 and 1877 she circumnavigated the world.

and **101** These two photographs show Victorian
[st]am yachting at its most luxurious. They were taken on
[boa]rd the *Victoria and Albert,* the Royal Yacht, in 1902, and
[sho]w respectively the main dining room and a cabin. A
[few] fragments of these opulent furnishings were preserved
[wh]en the vessel was broken up and can be seen
[rec]onstructed in diorama form in the new Yachting
[gall]eries at the National Maritime Museum.

102 And here is another survivor from the very end of
the era, the *Kyle* built in 1914, but entirely Edwardian in
her engineering and furnishings. She served as an ice-
breaking passenger and freight vessel in the railway
service on the coast of Newfoundland and Labrador for
many years. Today she still lies at Riverhead, Harbour
Grace, Newfoundland, driven right up into shallow water,
forlorn, abandoned and derelict. This photograph was
taken by one of the authors in March 1977 and with this
relic surviving from before the great divide of the First
World War this selection of photographs is appropriately
brought to an end.